Stitch your
Sandy

52 Tuesdays

A Quilt Journal

by

Sandy Gilreath

52 Tuesdays - A Quilt Journal
by
Sandra H. Gilreath

© 2016

ISBN - 978-0-9894116-2-2
Published by Sandspurhill (Marie J Amerson)
Macon, Georgia

Dedication

This volume is dedicated to stitchers everywhere who have their own stories to tell.

Sandy Gilreath

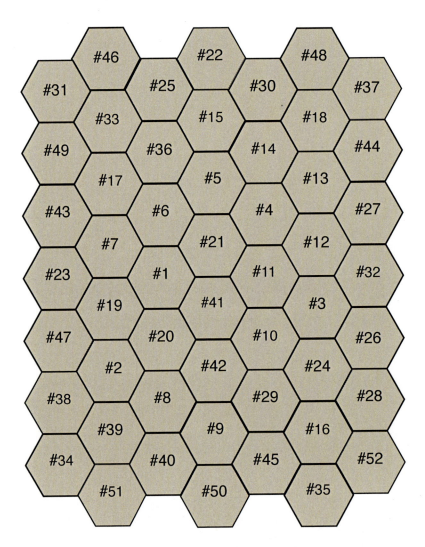

Key to the placement of
52 Tuesdays

52 Tuesdays - A Quilt Journal

Sandy Gilreath

52 Tuesdays - A Quilt Journal

Introduction

"Seeing and capturing ...things in the pages of a journal rescues them from the mundane. By giving attention and respect to small things, you raise them to a new level."
 - Cathy Johnson in her *Artist's Journal Workshop*.

Fifty-two Tuesdays is a quilt made up of smaller quilts. Every week for a year I made a small hexagonal quilt depicting some image from that week in my life. The following January, I hand stitched these units together, then machine quilted the joined edges over the bindings.

As I worked on each hexagon, I made notes about the inspiration for the image and recorded details about materials and techniques used. Each Tuesday night, I took a

Introduction

photo of the finished unit and added it to my written journal. That written record has become this book, the story of a quilt; the story of a quilt made of smaller quilts. Each small quilt has two stories to tell: one is about experiences in the everyday life of an ordinary person; the second is a story of using needle and thread to record those experiences.

People have asked, "Is this your original idea?" It is in that I haven't seen anything else exactly like it, but I realize no idea comes in isolation. Everything an artist does is based on something they've seen somewhere sometime. It is their combination of elements in a unique way that makes the artist's work different from others'. I saw the hexagonal layout in a quilt book. I've long known about the concept of using fabric to tell a story. But the idea of using events in my everyday life to include in this layout is mine. The selection of fabrics, techniques, and stitches are mine. I designed and created Fifty-two Tuesdays to represent a year of my life.

I have kept a journal in one form or another for more than thirty years. My initial journal entries were sporadic and limited to special events and travels. Over the years, my journals became daily entries with more creative writing, photos, and details of sewing experiences. In December 2014, I saw a photo of fifty-two hexagonal blocks joined together using crazy quilt embroidery and immediately knew I wanted to create a journal quilt with that format, combining my habit of journaling with my obsession with quiltmaking.

I did not appreciate the power of what I was creating until the fifty-two units were done and I looked back at them in chronological order. I asked my husband Jim to take high resolution photos of each quilt before I stitched them together. As I stood at my design wall and positioned the hexagons, I saw a year of my life pass before my eyes. Each image brought back memories of delightful days that might otherwise have been forgotten. Days that many would describe as mundane were now raised to a new level. For instance, I had forgotten that we saw a few flakes of snow in January until I saw the white french knots above the crow.

Each week found me looking for the perfect image to include. Sometimes I chose to preserve a scene from a place we had visited, other times one from a book I was reading. I included sample blocks from quilts I was making or sewing techniques I was exploring. I made a list of possible filler ideas, for when the well was dry, but that list was not needed. Instead, I found the challenge to be choosing the one image from several possibilities.

This Fifty-two Tuesdays venture turned out to be a sampler quilt, as well - a sampler of almost every material and technique in my repertoire. Most blocks used hand dyed solids for the backing or the background of the block, sometimes both. Background fabrics also included quilting cottons, recycled clothing, new and recycled linen, silk, and fabric pretreated for photo images. I used various battings, including wool, cotton, and cotton/polyester blend. A variety of threads, techniques, and embellishments made for an interesting year of learning and exploration. Each week's detail page includes specifics, and additional information is in "Construction Notes" following the journal pages.

I hope you find pleasure in some of the everyday images I included in the quilt. And if you are a sewist or a journalist, I hope you find inspiration to elevate your own everyday experiences by recording them somehow.

Introduction

Oh, and why Tuesday? Why not one of the other six days of the week? As soon as I saw the fascinating layout of hexagons in 2014, I immediately knew the title of my project would be "Fifty-two Somethings". I liked "Fifty-two Fridays" because of alliteration. But, alas, there were fifty-three Fridays in 2015, so "Fifty-two Tuesdays" sounded good to me.

52 Tuesdays - A Quilt Journal

January 2015

Tuesday #1

January 6, 2015

<u>Girl in Swing.</u>
During the recent Christmas season, I made numerous needlebooks as gifts for my stitching friends. I had fun thread sketching little girls with different hairstyles and varying dresses. I finally made a needlebook for myself today. She looks a lot like this one. So, to celebrate, I let her be the subject of my first miniquilt. Figures are stitched on linen fabric atop batting, then the edges frayed and fused to denim.

background: linen
technique: free motion quilting, raw edge appliqué
batting: 100% cotton
quilting thread: 100 weight silk

Writing on fabric:

Like needle books made for friends at Christmas '14. Now one for me!

January 2015

Tuesday #2

January 13, 2015

<u>Wool Crow</u>.
Jerry and Marie Amerson brought us a crow like this from A Pane in the Glass on St. Simons. I thought it a whimsical design, easily interpreted in wool. I had wool on my mind since I was preparing for the program at Heart of Georgia guild. The legs are bullion knots, snowflakes are french knots.

background: hand dyed cotton
technique: wool appliqué, free motion quilting
batting: 100% cotton
quilting thread: 60 weight polyester

Writing on fabric:
The crow is based on the one Jerry & Marie brought from A Pane in the Glass. Teaching wool appliqué this week at Heart of Ga Quilt Guild. We saw a few snowflakes.

January 2015

Tuesday #3

January 20, 2015

<u>Whimsical Elephant.</u>
Judy Shreve's artwork is on display at Macon Arts Alliance as part of their Whimsy exhibit. I love the purity and sparseness in her work. I bought a painting, "Walking Down a Country Lane, " but found her derby-wearing elephant in another work to be unforgettable.
Permission to use image in this quilt granted by Judy Shreve.

background: hand dyed cotton (pieced)
technique: wool appliqué, hand embroidery, free motion quilting
batting: 100% cotton
quilting thread: 100 weight silk

Writing on fabric:
Inspired by MAA "Whimsy" exhibit featuring work by Judy Shreve.

January 2015

Tuesday #4

January 27, 2015

<u>The Farm House.</u>
On Saturday and Sunday, we took drives on Georgia backroads and saw blue skies, sculptural trees, and farmhouses. Winter landscapes seem to reveal the skeletal structure of nature. On Saturday, we ate lunch at The Farm House in Ellerslie. This restaurant and gift shop are housed in an old sharecropper's cabin with rambling additions. Wandering guineas filled the farmyard with chatter.

background: hand dyed cotton
technique: raw edge appliqué, free motion embroidery/quilting
batting: 100% cotton
quilting thread: 50 weight/2 ply cotton

Writing on fabric:
Weekend drives on winter backroads—passed skeletal trees and farmhouses. Lunch at The Farm House in Ellerslie with guineas roaming.

February 2015

Tuesday #5

February 3, 2015

<u>Gee's Bend style quilt.</u>
I spent Superb Owl Sunday doing improvisational piecing much like Gee's Bend women would have done. I used a sunprint of Queen Anne's Lace, old shirts, favorite fabrics in blue and brown with a touch of green. This hexagon is a miniature version of the larger quilt using the same fabrics. Here, I used a commercial stencil to make the sunprint image of a quilt as the center. These sunprints were created using commercially pretreated cotton fabric.

background: pieced surround with Jim's old shirt
technique: improvisational piecing, hand quilting, button embellishments
batting: 100% cotton
quilting thread: cotton hand quilting

Writing on fabric:
Superb Owl Sunday at Gee's Bend. Jim's shirts, my shirts, favorite fabrics, sunprint, indigos. Cherrywood, green, and a little brown check!

February 2015

Tuesday #6

February 10, 2015

<u>Black and White House with Crow.</u>
Last Friday night was the opening of the Shades of Grey exhibit at Macon Arts Alliance where Linda Dease Smith's art group had their black and white work on display. Linda's work included a quilt made by my house pattern and a sculptured crow Jim helped stabilize.

background: Japanese woven taupe cotton
technique: needleturn appliqué, raw edge appliqué, free motion quilting
batting: wool
quilting thread: 100 weight silk, 50 weight/2 ply cotton

52 Tuesdays - A Quilt Journal

Writing on fabric:

From Shades of Grey exhibit at MAA included Linda's house quilt using my pattern. Jim helped with her crow sculpture.

February 2015

Tuesday #7

February 17, 2015

Blue Hearts.
I'd been making some blue hearts to put in a bowl just because I like them. We had a glorious Valentine's Day, so it seemed right to celebrate this week with blue hearts. Fabrics included wool, denim, and part of an old shirt of Jim's.

background: hand dyed cotton
technique: free motion quilting, appliqué, embroidery, buttons
batting: 100% cotton
quilting thread: 50 weight/2 ply cotton, 100 weight silk

Writing on fabric:
Blue Hearts. J R R Tolkein, Pandora, Glorious Valentine's Day

February 2015

Tuesday #8

February 24, 2015

<u>*Train Station.*</u>
Our friend Ken Clark died on Saturday, Feb 21. His 92 years were full of adventures; flying in WWII, acting, birding, and horse farming. The sign in our powder room ("Please do not flush toilet while train is in station") prompted a serenade when he visited us. I printed his obituary on fabric and cut out the train and station from that fabric. The tracks are cut from a printout of the lyrics and musical score from the song.

background: silk matka
technique: raw edge appliqué of custom printed fabric
batting: 100% cotton
quilting thread: 50 weight/2 ply cotton

Writing on fabric:
Ken Clark's Serenade

March 2015

Tuesday #9

March 3, 2015

Jan Patek House.

Many professional pattern designers inspire me. Jan Patek is one whose primitive designs lower my blood pressure. I've made the full size of this house pattern in summery colors, but this reduced version is so calm in Japanese fabrics. Doesn't it look welcoming on a cold evening?

background: linen
technique: needleturn appliqué, free motion quilting
batting: 100% cotton
quilting thread: 100 weight silk

Writing on fabric:
Jan Patek house—loving primitive houses, love Japanese woven!

March 2015

Tuesday #10

March 10, 2015

Shade Tree Mechanics.
This is a raw-edge free motion mockup of a larger quilt. Making this miniature version encourages me that the final product will be satisfactory. The full size quilt made to auction at the upcoming Vintage Chevrolet Club auction is a complex appliqué project which is still in progress.

background: tone-on-tone check
technique: raw-edge appliqué, thread sketching
batting: 100% cotton
quilting thread: assorted

Writing on fabric:
Shade Tree Mechanics

March 2015

Tuesday #11

March 17, 2015

<u>*Jude Hill Nine Patch.*</u>
The textile images and the poetry on the Spirit Cloth blog are stunning and soul soothing. I experimented with several of Jude Hill's techniques in this block using old fabrics of various textures.

background: hand dyed cotton
technique: hand piecing, hand embroidery, free motion machine quilting
batting: 100% cotton
quilting thread: 100 weight silk

Writing on fabric:
Jude Hill inspired. Paperless piecing. Invisible basting. Fabric beads.

March 2015

Tuesday #12

March 24, 2015

<u>*Curved Log Cabin.*</u>
This was the week members turned in curved log cabin blocks to Sheila Bender for our guild's raffle quilt for 2016. I made two of those blocks and then downsized the pattern to include here. The logs in the raffle quilt finished at 1" and 2". I shrunk them to 1/2" and 3/4" for this block. Batiks and Kona cotton are the same fabrics as used in the guild's quilt.

background: hand dyed cotton and batiks
technique: machine piecing and in-the-ditch straight line quilting
batting: 100% cotton
quilting thread: 50 weight/2 ply cotton, 60 weight polyester

Writing on fabric:
Curved log cabin blocks for guild raffle quilt.

March 2015

Tuesday #13

March 31, 2015

<u>Ty's Tours.</u>
In recent years, Jim and I have enjoyed several trips to Florida to enjoy bird photography with friends. To commemorate this trip, I printed a state map on fabric, then embroidered our route. I designated birding sites and quilt shops with french knots. A button maps a life bird sighting. The photo of leader Ty Ivey was taken by Jim Gilreath.

background: silk
technique: hand embroidery, free motion quilting, raw edge appliqué
batting: 100% cotton
quilting thread: 100 weight silk

Writing on fabric:

Ty's Tour 2015: Seven friends, photography, birding, music, laughter, sewing, shopping, eating, making memories.

April 2015

Tuesday #14

April 7, 2015

Parade Ready.
A wool floppy eared rabbit is appliquéd in wool. The stem and leaves are needleturn appliqué in cotton. A vintage button serves as a springtime flower. Rabbit inspired by work of Pam Manning.

background: hand dyed cotton
technique: wool appliqué, free motion quilting
batting: 100% cotton
quilting thread: 60 weight polyester

52 Tuesdays - A Quilt Journal

Writing on fabric:
Happy Easter!

# Tuesday #15

April 14, 2015

<u>*Clematis in Bloom.*</u>
Some weeks my Tuesday quilt is set in my mind or even completed by the preceding Friday. This is a week which was busy, with many potential images, but on Monday morning's walk, I realized, "I haven't made my hexagon yet". Then I saw the clematis blooms by the fence and had the design. Drizzle stitches serve as the stamens of the bloom.

background: hand dyed cotton
technique: needleturn appliqué, hand embroidery, free motion quilting
batting: 100% cotton
quilting thread: 50 weight/2 ply cotton

Writing on fabric:
Clematis in bloom.

April 2015

Tuesday #16

April 21, 2015

<u>Rainy Weather.</u>
Since we had rain every day for the past week (4.5 inches at our house) and gloomy, gloomy, days, this seemed to be a good visual symbol of the week.

background: hand dyed cotton
technique: fused appliqué, free motion quilting
batting: 100% cotton
quilting thread: 50 weight/2 ply cotton, 60 weight polyester

Writing on fabric:
>4" rain in past week
Great Sewing Weather!

Tuesday #17

April 28, 2015

<u>Deer in Woods.</u>
We've had good porch weather this week and being out in our favorite "room" a lot has meant we've seen our pet deer frequently. At least once a day, we've seen them - usually two, sometimes three - walking through the front yard. We keep the hostas sprayed and hope they don't eat a salad anytime soon.

background: "taupism" fabric with trees
technique: needleturn appliqué, free motion quilting
batting: 100% cotton
quilting thread: 100 weight silk

Writing on fabric:
We've seen deer in our yard every day this week. So far, no hosta salad.

Tuesday #18

May 5, 2015

<u>*Deliberately Irregular Hexagons.*</u>
The Japanese aesthetic in quiltmaking intrigues me. Work from Yoko Saito is especially appealing. I've been working a lot in the evenings on my version of her freeform hexagons. I dove into my collection of Japanese woven taupes and added some other fabrics which were similar in color. I began work on a new linen background fabric that was tricky to hand stitch, so turned to an old linen pillowcase. While working, I was inspired to add a red wool flower.

background: linen from pillowcase
technique: needleturn appliqué, wool appliqué, hand quilting
batting: 100% cotton
quilting thread: 40 weight/2 ply cotton

Writing on fabric:
Deliberately irregular hexagons.

May 2015

Tuesday #19

May 12, 2015

<u>*Queen Anne's Lace.*</u>
Our plants are blooming beautifully! That meant lots of choices for the week, but this sunprint won out. I enjoyed experimenting with thread sketching irregular edges atop the needleturn appliqué leaves. And, I made my first bee using Sue Spargo's bullion knots.

background: sunprinted cotton fabric
technique: needleturn appliqué, hand embroidery, free motion quilting
batting: 100% cotton
quilting thread: 100 weight silk

52 Tuesdays - A Quilt Journal

Writing on fabric:
Queen Anne's Lace is in bloom!

May 2015

Tuesday #20

May 19, 2015

<u>Wonky Star.</u>
In preparation for teaching a class at the July meeting of the Heart of Georgia Quilt Guild, I have completed four quilt tops using wonky star blocks in a variety of sizes. Fast, fun, and forgiving makes this a fun block to sew.

background: hand dyed cotton
technique: machine piecing, straight-line quilting with walking foot
batting: 100% cotton
quilting thread: 50 weight/2 ply cotton

Writing on fabric:
Wonky Stars straight line machine quilting. Four quilt tops ready for demo after guild meeting.

May 2015

Tuesday #21

May 26, 2015

<u>Beehive on Linen.</u>
One of my favorite motifs is the beehive. This background was pre-washed Moda linen, the beehive quilting cotton. A running stitch of perle cotton and some bee charms add detail. In honor of Memorial Day I added an embroidered flag.

background: linen, pre-washed
technique: needleturn appliqué, hand embroidery, free motion quilting
batting: wool
quilting thread: 50 weight/2 ply cotton

Writing on fabric:
Working with Linen (pre-washed). Memorial Day!

Tuesday #22

June 2, 2015

French Farmhouse.
The Nightingale by Kristen Hannah is a novel of two sisters living outside Paris during WWII. The house in which one of them lived is the inspiration for this week's design. Searching for the background fabric in my stash thinking, "I know I have some fabric with a Paris map on it," revealed many delightful surprises which I had forgotten. So many quilts, so little time!

background: Paris street map printed on quilting cotton
technique: needleturn appliqué (with Japanese woven), free motion appliqué,
      free motion quilting
batting: wool
quilting thread: 100 weight silk

52 Tuesdays - A Quilt Journal

Writing on fabric:
Kristin Hannah, "The Nightingale" Paris street map. Reading novel.

June 2015

Tuesday #23

June 9, 2015

<u>Pear.</u>
An upcoming class I'm teaching at Couture Sewing Center has me playing with gentle curves and few pieces in a design. My goal is to create something that beginners can complete in a three-hour class in needleturn appliqué. This is a reduced size of the class pattern I will use.

background: linen
technique: needleturn appliqué, free motion quilting
batting: 100% cotton
quilting thread: 50 weight/2 ply cotton

Writing on fabric:
Preparing class samples. Beginning needleturn appliqué.

Tuesday #24

June 16, 2015

How to Catch a Frog.
Heather Ross is now a quilt and fabric designer. In this delightful memoir, she writes of her childhood in Vermont living in an old abandoned schoolhouse, exploring the woods, and catching frogs for a local restaurant. DIY projects are interspersed. The wool appliquéd schoolhouse is inspired by some wool projects I remember seeing in an issue of Quiltmania magazine.

background: quilting cotton
technique: wool appliqué, free motion quilting, raw edge appliqué, frog button
batting: 100% cotton
quilting thread: 60 weight polyester

52 Tuesdays - A Quilt Journal

Writing on fabric:
"How to Catch a Frog". nature, schoolhouse, memoir, DIY

June 2015

Tuesday #25

June 23, 2015

<u>Linen Basket.</u>
A fat quarter pack of polka dot linen that Corinne ordered for me at Couture Sewing Center was the start of a fun wall quilt and this miniature version. I reduced 12" blocks in the "Big Bloomers" pattern from Quilt Soup to 6" blocks for my wall hanging. The block here is reduced to a 3" version.

background: linen
technique: machine piecing, free motion quilting
batting: 100% cotton
quilting thread: 60 weight polyester

Writing on fabric:
Linen Baskets. Polka Dots.

June 2015

Tuesday #26

June 30, 2015

<u>T-shirt Vine.</u>
Cleaning out closets gave me some old t-shirts to upcycle. Alabama Chanin's use of cotton knit fabric produces charming designs in clothing. I explored her raw edge appliqué and exposed knots with a vine and leaf design. Not a fan of standard t-shirt quilts, I love this technique of reusing the knits. My version used t-shirts on linen to make the quilting easier.

background: linen
technique: free motion quilting, raw edge appliqué
batting: 100% cotton
quilting thread: 100 weight silk

52 Tuesdays - A Quilt Journal

Writing on fabric:
Exploring Alabama Chanin. recycled t-shirt.

Tuesday #27

July 7, 2015

Fireworks.

Using a machine-embroidered fireworks motif from a vintage tea towel, this week's hexagon commemorates the July 4 evening with friends. The Iveys and Amersons had dinner here with us, then we all went to see fireworks at Idle Hour. Using a tea towel is especially significant since I gave guests tea towels with appliquéd pears in stars and stripes fabrics.

background: vintage linen tea towel
technique: machine embroidery, free motion quilting
batting: 100% cotton
quilting thread: 50 weight/2 ply cotton

Writing on fabric:
Friends, Flags, Fireworks.

July 2015

Tuesday #28

July 14, 2015

<u>Basket in Churn Dash.</u>
Assembling my basket blocks from the Piece 'n Plenty pattern has occupied several days this week. Several guild members are working on this pattern simultaneously. I've done lots of small baskets for a border, but think now I'll set the big baskets (there are nine) in blue churn dash blocks and use the small ones somewhere else. The basket image here is fussy cut from an old child's dress found while antiquing.

background: vintage linen tea towel
technique: machine embroidery, free motion quilting
batting: 100% cotton
quilting thread: 50 weight/2 ply cotton

52 Tuesdays - A Quilt Journal

Writing on fabric:
Blue Churn Dashes and Brown Baskets

Tuesday #29

July 21, 2015

Jim's Grackle Drawn by Mark Ballard.
Summer drawing sessions have been "bring your own photo." I carried some of Jim's bird photos for subjects, and Mark drew this boat-tailed grackle from one of them. I made a print of the drawing on silk fabric, then quilted it with the "pumpkin seed" design, drawing a grid on the fabric and free motion stitching the undulating curves. Permission to use image in this quilt granted by Mark Ballard.

background: silk
technique: free motion quilting
batting: wool
quilting thread: 100 weight silk

Writing on fabric:
Summertime drawing class with Mark. photo by Jim Gilreath

July 2015

Tuesday #30

July 28, 2015

<u>Corgi.</u>
This week has been focused on Tasha, our Pembroke Welsh Corgi. She has been weak, has eaten little, and is not responding to treatment for her kidney disease.

background: quilting cotton
technique: needleturn appliqué, wool appliqué, free motion quilting
batting: 100% cotton
quilting thread: 100 weight silk

Writing on fabric:
Corgi-focused life, healing, mending, loving Tasha-Girl

August 2015

Tuesday #31

August 4, 2015

<u>Ms. Brown's Flag.</u>
At Tiffany's request, I made a quilted flag for her classroom. I wrote the words to the Pledge of Allegiance on the white stripes. It's hard to believe school starts this week!

background: hand dyed cotton
technique: machine piecing, needleturn appliqué, free motion quilting
batting: 100% cotton
quilting thread: 50 weight/2 ply cotton

Writing on fabric:
Flag for Ms. Brown's classroom. Words to the Pledge of Allegiance written on white stripes.

August 2015

Tuesday #32

August 11, 2015

<u>*Appalachian Trail Block.*</u>
The mountains call us and we must go. Our annual trip to Amicalola State Park for the Gilreath reunion included a bit of walking on the AT approach, enjoying cool mountain scenery. As usual when being away from home, the days are filled with possible images for the week's hexagon. Having had my foot in a boot healing a fracture the previous year, I found wearing hiking boots to be the highlight of my trip.

background: cotton kerchief, bit of wool
technique: raw edge appliqué, free motion quilting
batting: 100% cotton
quilting thread: 100 weight silk

52 Tuesdays - A Quilt Journal

Writing on fabric:
Amicalola Falls State Park. Family reunion. LOVE walking in hiking boots.

August 2015

Tuesday #33

August 18, 2015

<u>Hummingbird.</u>
In order to "freeze the wings" in photos of hummingbirds in our yard, lots of flashes and tripods are necessary. We've had fun in the mornings and afternoons with friends on our porch and in our yard. Jim's elusive goal for several days was to get two birds in focus in one shot. Here is evidence of his success.

background: hand dyed cotton
technique: photo on cotton fabric, free motion quilting, raw edge appliqué
batting: wool
quilting thread: 100 weight silk

Writing on fabric:
Hummingbird School. Lots of men, lots of flashes, lots of fun.

August 2015

Tuesday #34

August 25, 2015

<u>Lone Chimney.</u>
Monroe, Georgia, has several antique malls in old mill buildings. It's one of our favorite haunts. On our route, this lone chimney is a familiar part of the landscape. It fascinates me, knowing the stories it could tell about families in the house that's no longer there, the cows in the pasture, and the traffic passing by.

background: hand dyed cotton, quilting cotton
technique: needleturn appliqué, raw edge appliqué, free motion quilting
batting: 100% cotton
quilting thread: 50 weight/2 ply cotton

Writing on fabric:
Antiquing in Monroe. My friend, the lone chimney, outside Monticello, an essential in the southern landscape.

September 2015

Tuesday #35

September 1, 2015

<u>Spool Block.</u>
This is a test block using stamps designed to print directly on fabric. I saw the stamps in a quilt magazine and thought it would be a great way to handle a hand piecing project, especially while traveling.

background: quilting cotton
technique: hand piecing, machine piecing, free motion quilting
batting: 100% cotton
quilting thread: 50 weight/2 ply cotton, 100 weight silk

Writing on fabric:
Spool block. Hand Piecing. Stamped templates.

September 2015

Tuesday #36

September 8, 2015

<u>Heart 'n Hand.</u>
We drove to Gainesville to visit our friends Bob and Harriet. I presented an evening trunk show of my quilts at the Heart 'n Hand guild in Dawsonville. The following day I taught a workshop making house, boat, and tree blocks using my stack and shuffle technique. Making new friends is a wonderful outcome of these teaching adventures.

background: linen (old jumper)
technique: needleturn appliqué, wool appliqué, free motion quilting
batting: cotton/polyester blend
quilting thread: 100 weight silk

Writing on fabric:
Heart 'n Hand Quilt Guild, Dawsonville. Trunk show.

September 2015

Tuesday #37

September 15, 2015

<u>Jude Hill Feather.</u>
I collected images of Jude Hill's fabric feathers long before I knew anything about her work. I've been playing with some of her feather techniques, black/white embroidery, and then the stripes. I love Kaffe Fassett's woven stripes!

background: hand dyed cotton
technique: hand piecing, needleturn appliqué, free motion quilting
 batting: 100% cotton
quilting thread: 100 weight silk

52 Tuesdays - A Quilt Journal

Writing on fabric:
Magic Feather. Spirit Cloth blog. Kaffe stripes.

Tuesday #38

September 22, 2015

<u>*LaPassacaglia Preview.*</u>
Tula Pink has a portion of the *LaPassacaglia* quilt on her design wall. When I saw it in a photo, I was entranced. I enjoy English paper piecing and I gave myself the precut paper pieces and the acrylic templates for my birthday. This is a sample of the star which was the most eye-catching element to me.

background: hand dyed cotton
technique: English Paper Piecing
batting: 100% cotton
quilting thread: 50 weight/2 ply cotton

Writing on fabric:
Preview of LaPassacaglia. English paper piecing. multiple shapes. fussy cutting motifs. bilateral symmetry.

September 2015

Tuesday #39

September 29, 2015

<u>Nancy Hanks.</u>
A steam locomotive reminiscent of the train that ran from Macon to Atlanta until 1972 was back in town. An engine from the Tennessee Valley Railroad Museum gave excursion rides this weekend. On Saturday, Jim & I rode to Gordon to take photos. On Sunday, we took the round trip excursion to Tennille with friends Jerry and Marie. The pieced block is one of many traditional blocks using the name "rail crossing".

background: hand dyed cotton
technique: machine piecing, free motion quilting
batting: 100% cotton
quilting thread: 50 weight/2 ply cotton

Writing on fabric:
Steam locomotive. Nancy Hanks. Gordon on Saturday, Tennille on Sunday. Through Georgia woods.

October 2015

Tuesday #40

October 6, 2015

<u>Cotton Boll.</u>
Cotton fields in full bloom, blue skies, a glorious fall day - all that's missing is some new fabric. Oh, wait, Marie and I took care of that, too. A fun outing and the best hamburgers in Hahira made for a memorable day in south Georgia!

background: hand dyed cotton
technique: wool appliqué, needleturn appliqué, free motion quilting
batting: 100% cotton
quilting thread: 50 weight/2 ply cotton

Writing on fabric:
Quilt Shop Hop for Two
Marie & I went to Moultrie and Hahira and enjoyed blue fall skies and cotton fields.

October 2015

Tuesday #41

October 13, 2015

<u>Goat Show.</u>
We made three trips to the Georgia National Fair in Perry this year. On the trip with Ty and Cathy we spent time in the goat barn and at a goat show. One of the most memorable sights was goats awaiting their turns to compete. Many of them were wearing sweaters to keep clean. There's a career opportunity - designing goat clothing.

background: hand dyed cotton
technique: drawing, needleturn appliqué
batting: 100% cotton
quilting thread: 100 weight silk

Writing on fabric:
Ga National Fair with Ty & Cathy. We saw a Goat Show. Narration by Tifton goat farmer Ray Phillips and family.

October 2015

Tuesday #42

October 20, 2015

<u>*Amerson River Park Pavillion.*</u>
One of our favorite places to go for a walk is this park. Through Ocmulgee Audubon Society, we have history walking here when it was inaccessible to the public without special permission and rustic trails were the only paths. Now it has paved walkways, picnic shelters, and a small playground. We have it pretty much to ourselves on weekday mornings. The natural setting of the woods and river are the main attractions; the beautiful stonework is fabulous, too.

background: old shirt of Jim's
technique: needleturn appliqué, free motion quilting
batting: wool
quilting thread: 100 weight silk, 50 weight/2 ply cotton

Writing on fabric:
Pavillion at Amerson River Park. Beautiful walking trails. Stonework. River.

October 2015

Tuesday #43

October 27, 2015

<u>Indian Springs Bridge.</u>
Early memories from our childhoods, memories from our dating days, and memories with our girls there make Indian Springs State Park a special place for Jim and me. This past Sunday was our latest visit there. The magic still exists.

background: linen
technique: free motion quilting, raw edge appliqué
batting: 100% cotton
quilting thread: 100 weight silk

52 Tuesdays - A Quilt Journal

Writing on fabric:
Indian Springs State Park. Glorious fall day. Trips down Memory Lanes.

November 2015

Tuesday #44

November 3, 2015

<u>*Pumpkin & Vine.*</u>
Pumpkins and scarecrows and black cats have been out and about at our house for the past month. The Jack 'o Lanterns that live on the front porch and inside the house are put away for now, but lots of pumpkins stay out until Thanksgiving.

background: Quilters' linen (cotton fabric)
technique: needleturn appliqué, hand embroidery
batting: 100% cotton
quilting thread: 50 weight/2 ply cotton

Writing on fabric:
Pumpkins still everywhere.

November 2015

Tuesday #45

November 10, 2015

<u>Gingko Leaves.</u>
Gingko leaves falling in puddles on green grass - one of my favorite scenes in fall. I confess to driving to visit special trees when I think the time is right. The prettiest ones this year have been in Rose Hill and Riverside Cemeteries. Our walks in the glorious fall days have been magical. Yes, in the cemeteries; and the artwork there is fabulous, too.

background: hand dyed cotton
technique: needleturn appliqué, free motion quilting
batting: 100% cotton
quilting thread: 50 weight/2 ply cotton, 100 weight silk

Writing on fabric:
Gingko leaves at Rose Hill. Walking, reading stones, telling stories.

November 2015

Tuesday #46

November 17, 2015

<u>**Denim Cathedral Windows.**</u>
Cathedral windows are a very impressive block. Couple the design with recycling denim, exposing raw edges, and using hand dyed cotton fabrics, and WOW. I must make this bigger, bigger, bigger.

background: hand dyed cotton
technique: machine piecing, raw edge machine appliqué, free motion quilting
batting: 100% cotton
quilting thread: 100 weight silk

Writing on fabric:
Cathedral Window. Denim. Hand Dyed Cotton.

Tuesday #47

November 24, 2015

<u>Appliqué & Embellishments.</u>
 I taught the third segment of a needleturn appliqué class at Couture Sewing Center on Saturday. We explored using rick rack, ruching, broderie perse, skinny stems, and beading. The fabrics in this miniature version are from the same collection we used in the class.

background: hand-dyed cotton
technique: needleturn appliqué, beading, free motion quilting
batting: 100% cotton
quilting thread: 100 weight silk, 50 weight/2 ply cotton

52 Tuesdays - A Quilt Journal

Writing on fabric:
Appliqué #3. Broderie perse, skinny stems, beading, and more!

December 2015

Tuesday #48

December 1, 2015

<u>*Donna's Front Door.*</u>
I am blessed with health, love, and happiness. It's easy to give thanks when there is so much to celebrate. Jim and I enjoyed holiday meals with all our family, but the meal on Thanksgiving Day ushered in a new era for us - a holiday meal as guests at our child's table. We had that meal with Donna in her new home. The meal and company were delightful! Her front door is depicted here.

background: quilting cotton including brown check
technique: reverse appliqué, piecing, free motion quilting
batting: 100% cotton
quilting thread: 50 weight/2 ply cotton

Writing on fabric:
Thanksgiving in Tifton with Donna, Connor, & Michael

December 2015

Tuesday #49

December 8, 2015

<u>Susan Lenz Signature Block.</u>
A recent episode of The Quilt Show featuring Susan Lenz amazed me. Further research into her work led me to her current exhibit in Carrollton at the Georgia Quilt and Textile Museum. Wow! A wonderful day filled with delight and inspiration. Old linens, lace, buttons, and crayon rubbing are all elements of Susan's work which I combined to add my monogram to this quilt The trip followed a route with many memories for Jim and me. We recounted old stories and laughter filled the car as we rolled along. It's such simple things that bring us joy. Once home, I pulled out old journals and read details of earlier trips to Sharpsburg and Newnan and Senoia, reaffirming the importance of the journaling process. Then on paper, now on cloth.

background: old shirt of Jim's
technique: free motion quilting, raw edge appliqué
batting: 100% cotton
quilting thread: 100 weight silk

Writing on fabric:
SE Quilt & Textile Museum. Work from Susan Lenz. crayon rubbings, vintage linens. Laughter and inspiration made the day!

December 2015

Tuesday #50

December 15, 2015

<u>Houses.</u>
At the December Christmas luncheon, guild members presented me with thirty-three house blocks to assemble into a memory quilt. What a precious gift from my quilting sisters: a puzzle, design, and stitching experience all in one! Sue Spargo fabric was the perfect choice...neighborhood established.

background: hand dyed cotton, commercial print (Sue Spargo design)
technique: improvisational piecing, free motion quilting
batting: 100% cotton
quilting thread: 50 weight/2 ply cotton

Writing on fabric:
"At Home With My Quilting Sisters" 33 house blocks were given to me at guild party. A neighborhood!

Tuesday #51

December 22, 2015

<u>Buttonwood Farm.</u>
I'm continuing work on the indigo and wool wall hanging using a Maggie Bonanomi pattern. At this point, I'm freely cutting leaves and blooms and adding them where I wish. I've learned to skip the template making step whenever I can. A primitive design is the perfect place to "eyeball it".

background: linen
technique: free motion quilting, raw edge appliqué
batting: 100% cotton
quilting thread: 100 weight silk

Writing on fabric:
Indigo fabrics, linen, and wool. All on "Buttonwood Farm"

December 2015

Tuesday #52

December 29, 2015

Christmas Tree.
In the last week we've celebrated the season with friends and family. A new tree is the center of our decorations this year, along with all our Santas. The tree is from a wool collection I received at Christmas.

background: hand dyed cotton
technique: wool appliqué, free motion quilting, button embellishment.
batting: 100% cotton
quilting thread: 100 weight silk

Writing on fabric:
A week filled with love, laughter, friends, and Family. Peace on Earth.

Construction Notes

This book is more of a "how I did it" than a "how-to do it" publication. Unlike many quilt books, this does not include templates and placement diagrams. Still, I hope to encourage you to explore ways to create your own journal quilt, so I am including some details about my stitching experience. I have tried to organize my thoughts by topic so you can quickly find my thoughts on a specific aspect of the quilt.

Inspiration:
I have long been inspired by other quiltmakers. I have amassed a multitude of ideas and techniques from my grandmother and women in my small hometown, fellow members of quilt guilds, and professional quilting teachers. With the internet in my hands, I can find more inspiration, techniques, and instruction than my brain can absorb. I watch online quilting broadcasts, read blogs and social media posts from quilters whose work I admire, and listen to podcast interviews with quiltmakers.

In my journal notes there are names of many fiber artists: Jude Hill, Maggie Bonanomi, Sue Spargo, Yoko Saito, and others. I encourage you to check out these experts online and you will see examples of their work with details of their techniques. In this section, I elaborate on some of these quiltmakers' work, but you will want to delve deeper. You may find a connection to some aspect of their work that I haven't noticed yet.

I find inspiration from artists in other mediums as well: paintings, drawings, photographs, carvings, pottery. In his fabulous Super Seminars, Ricky Tims teaches that quiltmakers should study another medium. Following such advice I find that Mark Ballard's drawing classes informed my work with traditional quilts, and they have flung the door wide open to the world of art quilts and mixed media.

Finding inspiration versus outright copying another's design is a complex issue for quiltmakers. I was careful to not use copyrighted images from others, and if I thought my work was unmistakably recognizable as that of another, I sought and received written permission from the originator to include it. Though I would not think you will want to recreate an exact copy of this quilt, if any of my images fit your own story, you have permission to copy them to make templates. The printed images are near the 6 1/2" hexagons used in my quilt.

Fifty-two Tuesdays came about because of an image I saw in a book published by Quiltmania: *Voyage author de la Laine* by de Ségolaine Schweitzer. I saw large hexagonal blocks assembled with crazy-quilt-like embroidery between the blocks. The blocks had each been backed and bound separately, and included a variety of motifs in the appliqué. The book was written in French and English, so space for detailed instructions were lacking. But that was fine with me, the photo was worth many thousands of words and thoughts and stitches. I recalled buying a set of acrylic templates, the Hickory Nut, that were perfect for this project.

The article did mention that 52 blocks were used in their layout. That resonated immediately as potential for a block-of-the-week journal quilt. And so it began.

Working style:
My work habits are what some people would call disorganized or haphazard or creative. I prefer the third label in that list. Whatever it's called, I work on several projects at one time, moving from one to the other based on portability, materials at hand, and whatever my muse directs.
Many blocks in Fifty-two Tuesdays came about because I spotted an image that cried out to be included in the quilt. In other cases, the block became a testing ground for a new technique I had wanted to explore (Alabama Chanin appliqué, for example). In the case of the Chevy truck, the block became a miniature preview of a larger quilt in progress. Seeing the image of the idea in cloth gave me momentum to finish it.

This quilt adventure led me to experiment with some techniques I had been anxious to try. Sometimes making that one unit was enough to whet my appetite for more exploration. Sometimes I learned on that one mini quilt that I was done with that particular technique.

Planning the design:
A full-sized paper template of the finished block worked well for sketching appliqué designs and to audition quilting stitches. The template helped me determine the size of a photo if I was resizing it, and to position appliqué pieces. I made a line drawing of the finished size of the hexagon using the Hickory Nut, marked a dotted line 1/2" inside that (the binding is actually about 3/8" wide, but I didn't want to worry about covering my writing), and made several copies.

I have a camera (my iPhone) with me at all times, so it's easy to have a visual record of something that inspires me, and sometimes I print the photos on fabric (with permission from the photographer).

Block Construction:
The acrylic template set I used is from Hickory Hill Quilts and comes in three sizes. I used the "extra-large" Hickory Nut set, which produces a finished 6 1/2" hexagon. These templates are available at http://www.hhqsewingcenter.com or your local quilt shop. You could certainly make your own hexagonal templates, as well.

For this project, I used the "quilt-as-you-go" technique - each hexagon was layered with batting and backing, quilted and bound before attaching to another. The backing for each hexagonal unit was cut larger than the quilt top and batting so that after quilting, the excess backing could be folded over and stitched to the front to form the binding.

I began by precutting some hexagons of each size (the inner hexagon for the quilt top, the outer for the backing). I later decided it was easier for me to oversize the fabrics for each. I marked the inner hexagon on my quilt top, marked another line 1/2" inside that (with a removable marker) to guide my journal writing. I made the quilt top (often appliqué within these guide lines), then wrote my journal notes on the fabric. I layered and quilted the piece, then used the Hickory Nut set to cut away the excess. A rotary cutter works for the outer edge, but nice sharp scissors were best for the top and batting.

There were occasions when I produced a few "blanks" for travel or if I was planning to hand quilt a piece. That process worked well, too.

Writing on fabric:
I love including writing on my quilts. I think it adds such a personal note. I add handwritten labels to all my quilts and several of my pieces have my writing on the front, too. I have tried many pens, but my favorite one to use is the extra fine Sharpie. I especially like the retractable ones. They write more smoothly for me than the others. And, a sheet of sandpaper underneath helps hold the fabric in place. In Fifty-two Tuesdays, I used a sepia-toned fine point Sharpie to write some journal notes on the fabric. In the case where I used silk matka as the background and could not write on it, I wrote on the finished binding. As the year progressed and I began thinking about how to assemble the units, I avoided silk matka and wool as backgrounds, so I wouldn't be covering my words with free motion quilting.

Printing photos on fabric:
I used a variety of fabrics for photos on fabric, but generally got the best results using commercially pretreated fabrics prepared for the printer. The pretreated silk fabrics are beautiful, but some of them are not colorfast; others are difficult to remove from the backing paper. Some of the cottons are hard to needle. Just read the package and

consider how you are handling the fabric before making your choice. Are you stitching by hand? Will the quilt be washed?

I also used my home computer to print photos on solid quilting cotton which I ironed on to freezer paper first. I don't get quite as sharp an image that way, but it was readily available, and it worked. I washed them and didn't have any bleeding of color.

Batting:
Since I delight in free motion machine quilting, I often use a flat cotton batting in my quilts. If I want the dimension of faux trapunto, I will choose wool batting. In this project, I treated each hexagon individually and used the batting best suited for the look of that miniquilt. Since these pieces were small, it was a great way to use up scraps from other quilts. The differing weights and thicknesses of the blocks could make assembly a bit challenging, if you are going for perfection. I wasn't. This whole experience was about the story more than the faultlessness of the final product.

Needleturn appliqué:
The techniques that I use and teach to accomplish needleturn applique are elements I've learned from many sources. I've taken classes from Anita Shackelford and find her books to be a good resource, especially for dimensional appliqué. I like the casual style of Linda Jenkins and Becky Goldsmith at Piece 'o Cake Designs. Their instructions are detailed, as well. If I use a template for an appliqué shape, I generally use freezer paper on top of fabric, mark around the template and remove the freezer paper before stitching. This produces a soft turned edge. If I'm repeating an image many times, I will use template plastic instead of making multiple freezer paper shapes. Lately, I've been skipping the step of template making all together; drawing

the leaf or flower petal directly on fabric freehand. Other times, I use my light box to trace the pattern directly onto the fabric.

Confession:
I am a fabric snob. And, I am a thread snob. I'm not spending my time working with a fabric that feels coarse or cheap. I won't bother with a thread that gnarls or breaks. I encourage you to experience using the best products you can find. It's supposed to be fun! I have also decided I'm old enough that I don't need to save treasured fabrics or accessories for a better project that might come along. I'm all about using the good stuff now.

Cotton fabrics:
The hand dyed cottons I used are from my stash. I have a basket filled with a mixture of luscious Cherrywood, Liberty Homestead, and Ricky Tims' hand dyed cottons. I wasn't always certain which one I had grabbed, thus the generic label in the annotation for each unit. These are all delicious to use, but they do have a higher thread count than commercial quilting cottons. Hand stitching the binding on each, then assembling the units by hand would have been easier with a softer fabric. I was willing to deal with that disadvantage to get the rich texture from those fabrics. And, since these fabrics are firm, the result is flat and stable. Of course, if I had been stitching the binding by machine, or attaching blocks in some other fashion, the thread count would not have been an issue.

Hand dyed fabrics are available at larger quilt shows and online. Some local shops have hand dyed fabrics. I usually prewash hand dyed fabrics with Synthropol in hot water. I once pre-washed all quilt fabric, but don't always do that now ("snobby" buyers can be a bit careless if they are only paying for the good stuff). I do still wash really dark fabrics and reds and oranges, and I throw in a dye catcher, too.

Wool:
I prefer to use felted wool rather than wool felt. There is a difference in how they are created and how they perform. The hand dyed wools available through quilt shops are delicious and ready to use. I also enjoy finding a treasure in a consignment shop, cutting it up and felting it myself. Most often I use Sue Spargo's technique of stitching the wool with a whip stitch using matching wool thread. I have used perle cotton and a blanket stitch, as Lisa Bongean of Primitive Gatherings does. I find that a thin cotton thread in a matching color does a great job on wool, too.

Embroidery:
I have been doing some embroidery in phases since I was a child. Cross-stitch on gingham, crewel embroidery, then counted cross-stitch, embroidery using silk ribbon and the latest: crazy quilt style embroidery from Judith Montano. Most of those influences show up in this quilt. The most powerful component of my embroidery work came from Sue Spargo's work. I have taken a class with her. But I learned the most while completing her Bird Dance block-of-the-month project in 2013. Working on that with her *Creative Stitching* book at my side was an intense learning experience.

Embellishments:
I have quite a stash of embellishments. From my journal entries, you know that Jim and I enjoy antiquing. All sorts of buttons and pins, vintage linens, old cotton rickrack, remnants of lace and embroidery often find their way home with me. But I

don't discriminate. I buy ribbons and buttons from the latest collections, too. If you want a unique look to your work, don't ignore the world of scrapbooking, art supply houses, and hardware stores.

With regard to Fifty-two Tuesdays, many of the buttons, beads, and other embellishments were added after the quilting was completed. If this quilt ever needs to be washed, those can be removed and then reattached.

Marking on fabric:
Quilters are always looking for the perfect mark that we can see instantly, then remove when the appliqué or quilting is completed. New tools are constantly being developed. I test a new brand before using it, to see that it is indeed visible and invisible at the appropriate time. I will share that using hand dyed cottons in this project, I learned what ghosting means. I saw an "after-image" when I steamed the markings away. It was more noticeable on some colors than on others. But once I realized I wasn't imagining it, I changed markers on those fabrics.

Piecing:
If a pieced pattern has inset seams, I prefer hand piecing. Otherwise, I piece on a sewing machine. In both cases, I use a sharp needle and fine (50 weight/2 ply) cotton thread.

Quilting:
I love hand-guided, free motion machine quilting. That is the technique I used on most hexagons in Fifty-two Tuesdays. Working these units into my "disorganized or haphazard or creative" life meant the bobbin thread and tension in my machine was

different from one week to the other depending on what big project I was quilting. Since I didn't want to change everything about my machine setup in order to quilt a 6" space, I usually selected threads for the top and bobbin which worked with the colors of the hexagon, but were the same weights as those the machine and needle were already handling. I did quilt a few hexagons by hand. Considering the size of the hexagons, that would have been easier many times, but I love the things I can do with the machine in free motion. Hand quilting is not my strong suit. When I am free motion quilting, I feel as though I'm dancing with my sewing machine

Assembling the units:
I stitched the hexagonal quilts together by hand using a tiny whip stitch and fine cotton thread. Using solids meant that these stitches were hard to hide. When there was high contrast between the colors of adjoining blocks, I auditioned several threads and chose the least visible one.

I like the look of hand embroidery stitches to attach the blocks and felt those seams needed a bit more stitching to hold them together. The layers of hand dyed cotton in the bindings as well as batting made my units too thick to make hand embroidery a pleasant experience. So I loaded the sewing machine with a fun variegated thread (one created by YLI to coordinate with Cherrywood fabrics), lowered the feed dogs, and stitched a vine and leaves amongst the honeycomb design. The bobbin thread was destined to show because of all the solids. So I used the same thread in the bobbin. When free motion quilting, variegated thread can look "muddy" if you backtrack; thus the thread choice influenced the design lines of the stitching.

<u>In summary:</u>
I am a big fan of precision in quiltmaking. I have studied and followed advice from Sally Collins and other technical experts. But in recent years, I have come to embrace the casual side of quiltmaking. Fifty-two Tuesdays was not designed to be in a competitive quilt show. It was about journaling in cloth, not perfect execution of an intricate quilt design, so the quilt became a mix of the precise and the informal. Each hexagonal unit is as close to the next in size and shape as I found it possible to make. When needleturn appliqué is used, my stitches are as nearly invisible as I can get them. There are also some raw edge components (I love frayed edges on denim and linen). My piecing shapes are cut straight, but grainline is often ignored. Let me repeat, "It's supposed to be fun."

In reading about historical quilts I find a kinship with women who found a way to tell their stories in cloth. In past generations, at least some of these artists must have felt some satisfaction in their abilities to express themselves in spite of the discrimination of the times. I wonder what future generations will think of the stories today's quiltmakers are telling.

Construction Notes

Musings

This book is a journal about a quilt, and since that quilt is a journal itself, you have seen one event per week of my life for a year. But I keep a more detailed written journal. In the editing process for this book, I reread not only the journal entries relevant to this quilt, but all my daily journal entries of 2015.

What follows are selected journal entries related to this quilt. Some include ideas that didn't materialize, some are snippets of an idea being born. Know that these are lifted from my journals as I typed them, unedited and "in the moment" thoughts. But perhaps they will give deeper insight into decisions I made about what to include and how.

December 10, 2014

Early morning. I am planning next year's quilt. Or one which will last all year....Fifty-two Tuesdays. I have been haunted by an image I saw in Quiltmania magazine earlier this year...of 52 hexagons joined together. It's a sort of quilt-as-you-go project in that you cut two hexagons...the large one is the backing and binding for the smaller. Insert a piece of batting and it's complete in itself. 52 units join nicely into a symmetrical design. I want it to be a sort of diary of 2015...the image for the week can be related to what I'm working on, what I'm thinking about, where I've been (think...image on fabric of bird photo while on Ty's Tours). The small size could allow for embellishment, fanciful quilting, even hand quilting....a label would be ready for the back of each to journal in words the events or the thinking. This has so many possibilities...even while working on other big projects...some blocks can be just quilting explorations, some fanciful machine sketching of stick figure girls...hey, there's an idea for a whole new quilt!

So, will the blocks be white, or off white, with blue binding? The binding on each block will act as sashing on the front. So, I think white blocks with indigo bindings would be interesting, but the real indigo fabric is hard to stitch by hand...and that's a lot of white.

Maybe a neutral background for each block with hand dyed bindings? All hand dyed fabrics?

Will blocks be assembled as they are completed? In horizontal rows? From the center out? If I can make all these decisions, I can go ahead and cut the inner and outer hexagons and the batting in 2014 so the blocks will be ready to go. Do I want to do that? Or make design decisions as I go? I think I'll start a few blocks and then decide about placement and arrangement.

January 17, 2015

So, I've entered this world. So far, I've been on schedule (or even early)...finishing before going to bed on Tuesday night. Finding ideas has not been a problem. Choosing just one for the week is the trick. I have ample ideas stored up for "quiet" weeks or for when the well is dry or repetitive.

As to the fabrics, I seem to have chosen Cherrywood as the major fabric. I've used it on the back of both I've finished and on the front of one of those. I'm thinking neutral colors (sort of in the vein of Japanese colors), soft, but the designs can stand out. I've written on the first two blocks, but know that won't always be desirable. When I use wool as the background (as I will to exhibit quilting stitches on wool), I won't be able to write on the front. I have some fabric ribbon I can attach with the annotation or write on the back. I'm keeping a spreadsheet and a journal of each block, so if it goes as planned, I'll have a book finished when the stitching is done.

February 22, 2015

I woke up this morning and realized it's Sunday and I haven't given much thought to the hexagon for my journal quilt this week. Of course, I could appliqué a blue truck, since I've been working on the quilt for the VCCA raffle. But I will be working on that next week, too, so that could be next week's block. And, since the curved log cabin blocks were given out at the guild meeting for our raffle quilt, I could easily piece a small curved log cabin block...but that could wait until a week in March preparing to turn those two in to Sheila. And, since Ken Clark died yesterday, we've been talking about his visit here when he came out of the bathroom singing. He saw the "please do not flush while the train is in the station," sign and was reminded of the lyrics to a song from a show he had been in. Jim found all the lyrics online. Until we read his obituary yesterday, we didn't realize that he had been an actor for two years before entering the military. Before becoming Colonel, he was part of General McArthur's air honor guard at the end of WWII. He was an amazing man. So I'm tempted to make this week's block be a train station as a tribute to Ken.

But I'm reading *A Spool of Blue Thread* by Anne Tyler. There's an easy image to include. I could appliqué that or make some pieced spool blocks…a good thing to remember for another week, maybe.

March 1, 2015

I've become Facebook friends with Maggie Bonanomi. I saw some of her earlier posts today in which she was posting some (maybe three) photos for each letter of the alphabet. "I" had a photo of indigo linens, an antique indenture document, and ironware. "J" showed journals, jugs, and jars. All things I love, too, by the way. So my brain translated that to a possible subject for another hexagon quilt….two images per letter would do, but maybe just a total of 52…I can't imagine anyone coming up with two images for z….maybe I'll start my list. Oh, I already have in my going to sleep alphabetical process.

And, many other possibilities abound for yearly journal type quilts:
52 plants in a garden
52 childhood memories
52 quotes from family or from famous people
52 math topics I taught (wouldn't "end behavior aerobics" be fun to thread sketch?)
52 pieces of clothing with a memory…appliqued in the shape of the clothing
52 family photos on fabric
52 cute little girls sketched on fabric
52 quilt blocks

March 11, 2015

This week's block is a mock up of the blue truck under shade trees that I'm donating to Jim's VCCA for their silent auction. My goals for this hexagonal project were that each block is inspired by something I'm doing or working on during the week. Since I've been working on this blue truck for a while, it seemed imperative to include it in a block. I'm glad I did because the finished block inspires me to keep going on the big quilt. Once the needleturn appliqué was done, I was worried about the whole idea. Every quilt I make has a point where I think, "what was I thinking?". So doing a raw-edge mock up of my whole plan helps to see that, "yes, this is working." I may have to do that more often.

March 18, 2015

The progress on the quilt blocks, on the half-page journal documentation, and on the plans to use varied techniques seems to be positive. This past week's block looks a little different, in that the whole background is colored. I printed Mark Ballard's drawing of apples (from the class I'm taking) on EQ's printable fabric. I had some silk on hand, but it took 24 hours' drying time and I wanted to get to the quilting process. Not the best decision. The fabric I used was EQ's cotton lawn which is supposed to be easy to needle. It's ok on the machine, but it is hard to stitch through by hand. I used it on the beehives I made for Donna using Daddy's workbook pages as a background and learned that lesson then. I must research a softer printable fabric for hand appliqué. This block only had to be needled when stitching down the binding, but it was still painful.

I'm not sure of the colors in this one in the overall design scheme of my quilt. I used a lime green (Mark's favorite color) for the backing fabric and I have a feeling it's not going to play well with others.

I've also been playing with some of the stitching techniques Jude Hill uses in her Spirit Cloth and other projects. I'm holding on to a nine patch that is the right size to use in one of these hexagons in case the apple block has to be replaced.

May 12, 2015

As this journey continues, the constant is difficulty choosing the theme of the week. For example, this week I have these options:
a pair of hiking boots...because I've really been immersed in the story of Cheryl Strayed's book, *Wild*.
Queen Anne's Lace because mine is now blooming, and I have sunprinted fabric on hand with Queen Anne's Lace.
Appliqué on linen...because I've been exploring the virtues of using washed vs unwashed linen as a background for appliqué; and the exploration turned out to be on linen hexagons that fit in the journal quilt.
Wonky stars...because I've been working on those blocks yet again this week in all sizes...preparing for the demonstration at guild next week and for the class in July.
A tree...to show the landscape theme of our drawing class this week.

And, as I work on my quilt with the self-imposed rule that it be relevant to my week's events. I'm thinking of dozens of other categories of things that would work in this setting of hexagons.

May 19, 2015

Once again, the list of possibilities is astounding! This week, a few caladiums have finally come up in the yard (most of my bulbs became chipmunk food, I think. I planted at least 40 bulbs right before two weeks of steady rain (see hexagonal block with umbrella to realize the magnitude of the wetness) and noticed even then that some of them were "mushy" right out of the bag. Lesson learned: don't buy packaged bulbs. Either select them individually...or if they don't come that way, wait until the plants are for sale. Save time and let the professionals start them. If that work is for rotten bulbs in the ground, no money is saved by buying bulbs). So with my drawing class skills handy, I drew a caladium leaf, and realized that somewhere I have some fabric with caladium bulbs printed on it....so this would be a great time to include the broderie perse technique.

And bluebirds are flying all around nesting for their second brood of this season, pileated woodpeckers are mating and nesting in our yard, friends brought us a gift of a stained glass tree made from bubbles....perfect model for a tree made of wool circles.

The past week was dry, so we spent afternoons watering our plants, so a watering can motif would be appropriate. We went to the Knoxville Jug Fest on Saturday and a piece of pottery would symbolize that event—especially the blue rooster I bought from Mike Ledford. I've been drawing and planning my medallion quilt for the challenge, I've been studying Jude Hill and her work intently. I've continued to explore applique on linen: pre-washed vs not. I've even explored it on hexagonal shaped blocks scaled for use in this quilt.

I read a Jack Reacher book this week featuring trains. A block depicting a train would certainly be appropriate in this quilt made near the site of the old Lorane station.

Any one of these events would inspire several possible blocks. Just one week's proof that finding a topic of inspiration is NOT a problem.

But I've been furiously working on wonky star quilt tops to have samples for this week's guild meeting....having now completed four tops in varying sizes and combinations of fabrics. So it seems appropriate that a wonky star should be the block motif. And, since I changed modes on the Bernina from the free-motion quilting to straight stitch so that I could piece the big blocks together, it's a good time to include the technique of straight line quilting. Once done, I have a block with a lot of light background. This will offset another one that has worried me for a while.... one with a lot of white. So it seems that with 52 blocks, there is opportunity to repeat elements so there are fewer spots that stop the eye.

I continue to think about assembling the blocks. I can't do that yet because I need to have many more done before I commit to a layout. But I think I can see that it's scrappy enough that I can begin assembly before the end of the year....maybe even planning the last few hexagons' color scheme (background and backing) ahead of time. And I could put groups of two and three together so that some of the embroidery is done ahead. The sample I saw in the Quiltmania publication used hand embroidery stitches to assemble much like the Sue Spargo stitches that I've learned. And that may be what I do, at least in some cases. But I've long thought that the machine's zig zag with invisible thread, or a decorative stitch with heavier thread, might speed up the assembly process. It has now occurred to me that I could assemble them with invisible thread and a zig-zag stitch, then free motion quilt my vine with tiny leaves to unify it. The free-motion option would give me a lot more flexibility to cover less than perfect stitches in the bindings, Oh, oh, oh. I could free motion COUCH with a lovely yarn.

Now I'm excited! So I need to make some dummy blocks, assemble, and practice the free motion assembly part.

July 9, 2105

It's the middle of the night (well, 5:00 a.m..) and I'm awake thinking of the very concept I last wrote about. Lots more blocks are done and ideas are still swimming. One Monday morning as I was on my walk, I realized "it's Monday and I haven't made my block yet". Then I saw it. The first bloom on a *Clematis* for the year. So. That's how this happens sometimes.

Yesterday I applied a binding to a big quilt using the machine's serpentine stitch. It went so well that I'm thinking now would be a good time to make those dummy blocks and practice my assembly techniques. At times during the year, I think, "I must get busy or I won't have anything spectacular for our quilt show." Then I remember this project. I am determined to have it hanging in the show in mid-March. But that won't happen if I have to do all the assembly and embellishment by hand after January 1.

August 11, 2015

We went to north Georgia mountains last week, headed to the Gilreath reunion. An extra couple of days in Blue Ridge were nice, and there were many images there that spoke "Tuesday" to me. (flying pig, waterfalls, crows, to name a few). But the prevailing thought for me was joy in walking about in normal shoes. Sandals, tennis shoes, and, yes, hiking boots. Last year on this trip, I was using a cane or walking

stick, wearing a boot while a stress fracture in my right foot was continuing to heal. It was total delight to be free of that encumbrance and to be able to walk, walk, walk!

September 22, 2015

The weeks have continued to move by in our lives, busy with an ailing pup, travel, and classes. All events contribute to a big hexagonal quilt. The problem, if there is one, continues to be weeks with so many images that it's hard to choose one. I've been teaching classes, preparing new patterns to teach more, taking classes (drawing) and exploring new techniques. All provide ideas for hexagonal blocks. And, I find myself thinking ahead...when should I do "this" to be sure to include it in a block. Planning my schedule so I have a hexagonal space to put it. Like, the clock tower at the fair in Perry. If the week I delivered my quilt is too busy, then it can go in the week the fair is judged, or the week we go to the fair, or....?

December 4, 2015

I'm now reading *Flight Behavior* by Barbara Kingsolver. I identified with the main character Dellarobia. I've been to her church. I've met some of those people. I realize that she is living a life that I escaped. Not that I was that trapped into an impoverished rural existence, but I saw that around me and I could have lived that life.

The book has made such an impression on me. I see myself in her when a friend tells her that "well, you don't put up with much," when Dellarobia inquired why people thought she hated everyone. It seems I need to include an image from this book in my journal quilt.

So, what week will have a butterfly…when I finish reading the book? But there is Christmas stuff going on, too. If I can't fit in all the images I've conjured up this year (like the tower at the fairgrounds, the pavilion at Georgia College, Jim's butterflies), must I do this again in 2016?

December 5, 2015

My copy of *The Uncommon Quilter* by Jeanne Williamson arrived in the mail today. I had ordered it when I read that this book (specifically the grave rubbing technique she espouses) inspired Susan Lenz to go in the direction she went. I had never heard of either woman or their techniques when I started my "52 Tuesdays" adventure, but it is astonishing how my diary quilt parallels that of Williamson.

She challenged herself to create one quilt a week for a year. She did that, making all quilts 8" x 10" for the first year, with a Saturday night midnight deadline. She might have used less tedious (read traditional) processes in some of her pieces than I did, and she followed the rule of never discarding a quilt because it did not meet her expectations. But much of our experience is the same. Is this further proof that nothing new is under the sun? What we think is an original idea is just a different interpretation of one we had not heard about before, but that someone else, maybe many someones, is approaching simultaneously.

The kinship I feel with these strangers through my exploration and growth is amazing. I have never met either woman, but feel that we share so much. The same is true with Jude Hill.

Even the name the Uncommon Quilter gives me pause for thought. Back in the early days of my thinking that I might want a cute name for a pattern company or blog, I tossed around so many ideas...but the most recent concept came from one of my appliqué students. in an email to me, she encouraged me to write a book and include my rogue approach to appliqué and quilt making. She was referring to my casual placement of appliqué pieces and my openness to try different things. So a blog could be from the rogue quilter.

I have tried to resist the temptation to remake blocks of my quilt that don't quite meet up to expectations, but I have considered the overall look of the quilt and reserve the right to create a cohesive whole. The first block I made using a drawing by Mark Ballard was fine on its own, but the binding fabric I used on it was appropriate for that block, but garish when put on the design wall with others. I later used another one of his drawings in the quilt and planned all along to replace that first one with another image for that week. And there is one which has a silk matka background, so I wrote the journal entry on the binding fabric. With my plan to use machine couching to assemble the blocks, I'm not sure that will stand.

December 8, 2015

Once we drove to the Southeastern Quilt and Textile Museum last Thursday, I knew that something of Susan Lenz's work would find its way into this weeks' block. I had been fascinated by her crayon rubbings in the cemeteries, and had even tried that and planned a "Rose Hill Ramble" quilt for 2016. But even after watching her videos online and reading about her work in detail, I was unprepared for the magnitude of the impact her work would have. The script written in thread (free motion machine stitching on sheer fabric) was totally mind blowing. And, having tried to photograph a friend's quilt with embroidery on sheer fabric, I know why that particular installation is not shown on her website or videos. The paper "books of the dead" were impressive, too. And, the number of pieces was astonishing! The pieces of clothing used in their entirety with crayon rubbings on them were especially effective. As was the unbelievable number of buttons she had used. Wow!

There were other facets of the day that were worth memorializing in cloth, too. The "redneck roundabout", the plans to make this an overnight trip next time (because it is a "bring your lunch" journey from here to there), the antique stores, the memories of our first trip to Senoia and Sharpsburg and Collector's Corner, the anticipation and then the discovery of the "extra lodge" Jim and I had first seen in 1985, made this a treasured day of memories worthy of an entire quilt on its own. Once home, I dug out my old journal and read of our first journey to that part of the state. Jim and I both thrilled to the details I had recorded, but that we had forgotten. Just another reminder of how precious journals, and now journal quilts, can be.

January 2, 2016

I have no plans to continue the 52 Tuesdays format of a quilt per week in 2016. But I do understand why Jeanne Williamson did something like this for 7 years. Even though the 52 block was completed some 10 days ago, I find myself planning hexagonal blocks that would represent something we were doing. Champagne glasses, dancing, musical notes…. It will be hard not to continue selecting one image per week to put in cloth.

If I were to do it again, I would probably choose a different format...just to make the 52 Wednesdays have a different appearance. Squares, rectangles, whole cloth with images appliquéd on directly, who knows?

January 6, 2016

It's official. I'm doing this again. The "visual image of the week" has become part of me now. Since completing the Christmas tree block, I find myself looking for the image of the week. It feels like something is missing to think I'm not doing this anymore. Even Jim has said, "you could use this on a block this week." So, this process is not just part of me. It's part of us.

And, before I began stitching the 2015 blocks together, Jim made a high resolution image of each block. As I placed each block on the design wall in chronological order for its photograph, I saw last year pass before my eyes. Literally. It was a powerful experience to revisit those memories through the blocks I had made. I had forgotten that we had some snowflakes during January until I saw the french knots on the block with the crow. Yes, I will continue this.

"Fifty-two Wednesdays" has begun.

Musings

Final Thoughts

Though many days may seem mundane, it is the cumulative process of living those days that make life unique. I take joy in living a simple life. Some days are busy, some are quiet. All are treasures.

Rereading my journals for this process, and revisiting old ones on trips down memory lane, reinforced to me how valuable it is to keep a journal. Though I have been disciplined about writing things down, I have not often reread them unless I needed to recover details about an outing or a family treasure. In order to savor memories, you must revisit them.

And, so, I am resolved to continue the journaling process. Now I am attempting to include more sketches and illustrations in my written records. Assembling this quilt has emphasized that having a visual representation of a memory makes it easier to retrieve the joy of the moment.

My textile journal is continuing, too. As Fifty-two Tuesdays was completed, I realized I couldn't not do this again. Like many other experiences, doing it once taught me a lot, part of which was what I yet had to learn.

I recently made the acquaintance of a new quilting friend. In sharing photos of the types of quilts we make, she saw Fifty-two Tuesdays. This stranger-yet-sister told me about memory quilts she made for family members, using techniques similar to mine. She loved my journal quilt and said, "I'd like to do that. May I steal your idea?" I replied, "Of course you should do it. You don't have to steal the idea. I'm freely giving it to you."

That's why I wrote about Fifty-two Tuesdays. I hope that other quiltmakers might find a way to add elements of their lives into the quilts they make.

I hope that you find something here to inspire you. If you have never kept a journal, give it a try. On paper, with drawings, on fabric, or a combination of any of those. I'd love to see what you create!

Sandy

52 Tuesdays - A Quilt Journal

Acknowledgements

This quilt would not exist without the experiences that shaped it. So the first thank you goes to my husband and soulmate, Jim, who is by my side in this life's journey. Many blocks in this quilt are results of sights seen on day trips antiquing, birding, or just "riding about". Jim's support for my passion is unwavering. He offers favorable comments on completed projects and those in progress, he travels to quilt shows and museums. He has encouraged me to stay involved with my writing group and my drawing group, noting the impact he sees those groups make on my work. His willingness to pause the tv while I run upstairs to get a forgotten spool of thread or another bit of fabric, his live guitar music while I'm sewing, his reminders to stop and smell the air outside, all help make my journey smooth. In addition, Jim's own passion for photography got a workout in this project. Thank you, Love.

To members of my writing group - Marie Amerson, Sandy Flatau, and Jim Ferrari - thank you for your encouragement to pursue this project as both a written journal and a story quilt. The questions you asked gave me pause to think about the next step. And your expectation there would indeed be a written product ensured that there is one.

To the friends who are part of my drawing group with Mark Ballard - thank you for your interest and support as this project progressed. Special thanks, Mark, for establishing this community of artists and for the image you permitted me to include.

To the members of the Heart of Georgia Quilt Guild - thank you for your passion for the art of quiltmaking, your expertise with all techniques, your ready answers to my questions, and our loving sisterhood. The quilt maker I am today is because of my association with you.

The only sister stitchers in my life who knew of this project were Marie Amerson and Donna Haman. They shared in the stories that led to the blocks that led to the quilt and listened as I pondered aloud some of the construction techniques. To Marie and to Donna, I thank you for unending support.

Other family members - Tiffany and Kenny, Ty and Cathy, and Jerry - knew of the project and asked for updates, keeping me grounded. Thank you all; your encouragement did not go unnoticed.

The quilt was easy. I do that. The journaling was routine. I do that, too. But assembling it into publishable format that is pleasing to the eye? That I do not do. My experience with layout and editing is best seen in test format, and that is not considered pleasing to many eyes. Enter Marie Amerson. Marie had experience with publishing, both print and digital books, and she was willing to learn more about layout and photo editing in order to make my work presentable. When she sent me a draft with that little crow dancing across the page, I knew we had a collaboration. So, to Marie, dear friend, Thank You.

52 Tuesdays - A Quilt Journal

Sandy Gilreath, Quiltmaker

Sandy grew up in a household where all women were always busy. If they were sitting, some sort of needlework was in the hands of her mother, her grandmother, her great-aunt, all of whom lived with her at one time or another. After a left-brain focused career in education, Sandy began to explore her creative side. Her rebellious nature continues to feed her work as she fearlessly explores more and more avenues to combine with fabric and thread.

Sandy has worked in traditional quilt techniques of piecing and appliqué in cotton and wool. Non-traditional works include photographs, blueprints, and mixed media. Her latest additions include crayon rubbings and original drawings on fabric.

Sandy has studied with numerous expert quilt makers including Sue Spargo, Karen Stone, Hollis Chatelain, and Ricky Tims. Artists Kaffe Fassett and Mark Ballard have also been her teachers. You will see influences of all these experts in Sandy's work.

Made in the USA
San Bernardino, CA
29 March 2016